deboning
a dragon

deboning a dragon

JULIE HARTLEY

Mansfield Press

Toronto 2019

Printed in Canada

Library and Archives Canada Cataloguing in Publication

Title: Deboning a dragon / Julie Hartley.
Names: Hartley, Julie, 1968- author.
Description: Poems.
Identifiers: Canadiana 2019019037X | ISBN 9781771262323 (softcover)
Classification: LCC PS8615.A77367 D43 2019 | DDC C811/.6—dc23

Editor for the press: Stuart Ross
Cover design: Denis De Klerck
Cover image: Friedrich Johann Justin Bertuch
Typesetting: Stuart Ross
Author photo: Craig Hartley

The publication of *deboning a dragon* has been generously supported by the Canada Council for the Arts and the Ontario Arts Council.

Canada Council for the Arts Conseil des Arts du Canada
ONTARIO ARTS COUNCIL CONSEIL DES ARTS DE L'ONTARIO

Mansfield Press Inc.
25 Mansfield Avenue, Toronto, Ontario, Canada M6J 2A9
Publisher: Denis De Klerck
www.mansfieldpress.net

Contents

i. fighting to fly

ii. winging it

iii. fewmets and flames

iv. dragon dance

i.

fighting
to
fly

contradicting faith

This woman
with Parkinson's
is the mother
of a long-distance runner
in training
– he speeds up
as she slows down –
and this man
seven feet tall
has an unborn daughter
just seven inches long:

they think about this,
these lovers pushing bicycles
he almost sixty
clutching twenty-one candles
for her birthday cake,
and pause on the bridge
to watch a teenage nun
glide over the frozen lake:
a single piano key
the sun plays
with one finger

all things are possible
even they are possible
while the blades of
a beautiful nun
write rapture
even in an
absence
of god

r.i.p.

hopefully
you have begun
your final death:
a monster princess
roaming the city
in a red-eye dark,
your bed so old,
without miracles,
fist-scrunching
the almost-blanket
of you

your skin snows
upon unborn daughters
descending the staircase
of graduation dreams
wearing ball gowns
of hospital green

elevated
to an end of life
and unreachable
you dwell in high places
half-alive, where
music scratches out
a sunset of roses; only
from down here
roses are bruises
and this the music
of thorns torn across skin

there is wispy hair
in the pain-howl
hollow of your neck
but nothing on the
bleached-bone hollow
of your head

and the doctors
are slowing down;
the pathway from
gurney to doorway
a circuit of sinkholes
and within this
puckered
plague-pocked earth
you are spoon-stirred,
dissolving;
icing sugar on a sweet bun,
windblown by the clatter
of an opening door
and drawn into nothing,
like a spring melt or
the snuffing out of self
in this sorrowful
season of serenity

Clown Queen

What you see here is a
bunch of child-balloons
bright-ribboned, deflated
as puckered bellies,
crow-winged and caught,
flapping from wires outside
the window of a girl who
let go. The child's face is
pressed into the disappointment
of a grey day, her flat nose
a gravestone. There is a
woman on the street
below balloons, beneath the
window, who is England's
Queen. Head held aloft,
one hand hooked onto fox-skin
bag and twisting in a royal wave,
she is propelled by invisible
corgis. The Queen pauses
beneath the television screen
of the child's window and
switches channels. In the window,
gravestone nose becomes a trunk
so long it curls in fossil whorls
against window glass in a hoped-for
glass smashing, a mournful
reaching out for lost balloons.
The Queen switches channels.
Now the balloons are a
nest of ostriches and the child
one of those monkeys with
suction hands sticking to glass.

The Queen switches channels
and the child is a slug. The slug
it will become in
thirty years, sloth-sunk
into sofas, waving the
munched leaf of a TV remote.
The Queen switches channels
and the child is a baby ostrich
trapped the wrong side of the
glass, blinking. The ostrich blinks.
Down in the street now
a multicoloured clown is held aloft
by a grape-bunch of bright
balloons, dancing on helium
air, bayed at by foxes, propelled
by a cart-pull of corgis. Here.
Look. Do you see?
The clown-queen tightropes
between telegraph poles
outside the nose-pressing
window of a child.

Child, Going Away

1.

tugged out of sleep and some lips moving, a baby brother moving, suitcases, clothes flying and chicken legs slipped from pyjamas, cold in thin shorts and the dad whispers: shh! don't wake the neighbours – something bad will happen if they wake the neighbours – and a pounding downstairs below a backwards brother shoulder-slung and they did not sleep, she can see by the empty wine bottle and the parent giggles dust-dropped in corners that they did not sleep, by the slobber-wet taste of wine on her breath when she kisses and she is giggling between whispers, this 3 a.m. mother who is adult-strange, while the girl pads barefoot through the black mist of a hushed garden by a shivering dog that bark-howls once and is silenced then they are stuffed into back seats like cushions, the dog is stuffed into back seats like a cushion and they are a hot stink of bare legs and sleep sweat, sinking down into a driving night that wraps them in its hum and pull so that sleep is a rope strung out before them, a firework-dance of headlights on a vinyl roof and she will always remember how the headlights fell into the bumps in the vinyl like sea spume into rock pools, pooling, and then the hot breath of brother snore and the way she learned the dog kicks in his dreams

2.

Waking to the bleed of sunrise in a stopped car. Cereal from boxes, without milk. He forgot the milk. You forgot milk! And they argue, because he forgot the milk. Soured skin, slackening, scented with sadness. He strokes the wolf tattoo on his upper arm. The wolf is a puppy now, sleeping in its nest of hairs. Beyond the dawn damp of windows, a sudden drop to grey sea and strangeness. A wind shivers, the bland nothing of a land erased. Inside the car, a pressing of noses and fingers. Misted glass, baby wail and a face-whip of dog tail. She thinks: how easily this life cliff-plummets to a loss. How easily, in the puppy eyes on an inner arm or a half-whispered: you forgot milk! a parent curl-sobs to a child. The girl is puppy-lost in the soured milk of this new day, and the future's fangs devour her.

3.

Outside the door and just beyond bare legs and inside the door and just beyond bare legs a known world drops off to a drowning.

Home Address

I come from Brixham summers: jellied eels on the beach,
swingboats, donkeys, knickerbockerglories.
I come from Sunday drives in the Scimitar,
homemade skirts we princess-spread on seats.
I come from the fat-crackle of Mabel's fish 'n' chips
ordered with our chins on the greasy counter,
eaten bare-kneed beside hairy great-aunts in the sun.
I come from unsuccessful pets: howling setters,
biting rabbits, budgies found feet up, canary chicks
roasting in the rear window of a July afternoon.
I come from a joyful getting lost on Haworth Moor
knee-high in purple heather, every time we did those hikes,
and afterwards, Heinz baked beans on pikelets
or Marmite thick-spread on baps. I come from raging
earache, deafness needle-sharp, whip-scarred warnings,
endless twilight longing, Romany persecution, steelworks
belching fire and nine brave fathers molten metal dead.

Otitis

See the growth on this head
a quarter-moon from the nose:
serpentine as sea cucumber
sponge-flinching from an almost
touch, stroked by a mind,
poodle-petted, running with tides
that sigh. Heartless at the centre
of this great world's heart, it moves
to the scent of a persistent throb:
mute music falling on deaf ear.

There is comfort now, sinking
into silence. Here, a room of one's own,
though lost in needle-spikes of pain:
big enough for tomes or tombs,
small enough to slip into an ear –
seaweeded entry to an underwater
cave. Beyond the place of too many
eyes, doubts pearl-bloom in a dark
and those random wrongs hurry
homeward, sponge-soft,
coral-candied. All this mouth can do –
half an eclipsed sun from the source
of peace – is ease back into brief
black-hole relief, and disappear.

Burn Off, '88

With the sudden turnoff of engine there is
hope-charged silence and darkness seeps in
through the cracks in the car; through
the half-closed windows of my mother's

Mini, piles up on seats, splits between knees,
sand-slips through swelled lips and
you say I love you, I say how hot it is
tonight, and when a hand slides slowly to a

skirted knee I open a door to let the heavy dark
outpour. And this is a hill. A tree-shiver
hill looking down on Hades; this counting of
six pines is the number of the beast. This beast

hunkers far below, belching out false
starlight while hard-hatted men ant-crawl
through hell. I say: *the explosion killed them*
but it didn't kill us. Beside me, you ponder

this revelation. Revel in our immortality.
A hand slips across shoulder, fingers fold
across bone and there is fire, Meatloaf screaming
in the car, bats bursting from a teenage

thrill-hell, but for now only the world sinks to
insanity. An angel-battalion of cloud marches
on a bootblack sky and the steelworks belch. Flames
arch into dark, burn, gorge themselves, lick, spit,

and guzzle. We wait for mushrooms and a flesh
burning. Instead, there is a dying back to black.

Not today. For now, just the scurrying, hard-hatted
men and the overarching angels of a someday

death. We will grow wings soon and join the war.
Face flamed, you breathe: beautiful.
And the headlights fizzle, hell bats fly,
fires burn, and dark night pours

upon us, weighs us with shackles
we will drag-rattle behind us on
a descent into knowing, into Doomsday,
driving the long, heavy road back to town

Neil Diamond, Coughing

This was his cassette, the casing marked
with the imprint of unbloodied fingers, the spool tight
from too much rewinding. A residue of coal dust.
Scent of the Old Spice we bought for his last birthday.

Playing the cassette, days after, I thought of him
sinking into static; white car wriggling into whiteout
like a leg pulled through a stocking or a bullet
shock-slowed by snow. He would have been singing
through that white-dark night as he moved toward
a reckoning. "Love on the Rocks" – we even know the song.
Tapping the steering wheel. Watched by white owls in trees.
His steak and chips waiting, down the pub.

Neil Diamond's foam voice filled the space between
hard windshield and soft brain in the slow seconds
just before. Filled the space between coal conveyors
on a snow-swept moor, and my mother. He thought
of her, or owls, or coal, as the tractor rolled over his head.

And all there is, for the rolling up and over,
is a single missed beat. A polite singer-cough,
mouth turned from mic as if in pity;
a jump, a fault, a hesitation. Such a minuscule wavering,
then the song wound on through its own white oblivion.

She handed me the cassette, her blue bulk blocking
a view of crushed car. Said: perhaps you'd like this
as if it was a souvenir. Standing on his ridge, back to
the buckled metal, listening to the dripping
of spring melt and squinting for owls in trees,
I stumbled through a whiteout as he had,

filling it with snow-buzz, steaks, coal –
anything but that too-polite cough,
the bent-head nod to a tractor rolling up
and over. I tried not to think of metal
smashing sideways to a face. Of his solitary
packing of snow up a shattered nose,
to survive. Of his raw steak, congealing.
Waiting like a jilted lover. Flesh cold. Forsaken.

There Were Drugs Involved

For a moment I am
caught in her vortex,
this splay-limbed, roll-eyed girl:
in a fractured mind
in a dirty bed
in a crumbling warehouse
on a ravaged waste ground
in a city
bombed.
I am in her mind
and in this shattered mind-mosaic
is a vortex spray-painted
on cracked plaster
here above this floating bed
and in this splattered vortex
is a split-apart mind.
I am her mind
spinning a bed-clutching ride
below a greasy boy who jump-zips
black hair into skintight jeans.
I am her mind
as it floats on the lake of its body
to a window, lichen hair
drifting downward,
petals from a window box.
Her mind always liked
a pound of Queensrÿche
a pint of vodka
anything to send her
skyward
and after that
I am not in her mind

and soon it is the sober
white-faced morning where
we are a line of grunt-sighing
shame and she is crumpled
with fright of her wild flight
and the policeman is stealing
her arm as he asks, kindly:
were there drugs involved?

Thin Lizzy

for Phil 1 & 2

> "Phil Lynott, the former lead singer of the rock band Thin Lizzy, has died... The 36-year-old rock star had been admitted to Salisbury hospital in Wiltshire on Christmas day after he collapsed from a drink and drug binge."
>
> – BBC, 4 January 1986

1

Life-estranged,
at least a cathedral
hung in his window.

2

We have no cathedral
to give you. Winter branches
whip-crack against the wall.
Your view is a mess of wet brick
and cold city squirrels.

1

Wife-estranged,
you waited as she plowed
through your night, tires skidding
in her half-frozen tears.

2

We are not a wife
but can scrub the evidence
of blood and bourbon,
crumple you like old money,
drive you through
the darkness of a pain.

1

Child-estranged,
at least his small ones
mourned on the frost
of each passing
Christmas day.

2

Your daughter
is gone.

1

Song-estranged,
he made a go of it
alone. The model said
he put on weight and
looked the better for it –
shedding music as
the pounds piled on.

2

Day 3, I feed you
a mess of eggs and steak
with a crumbled cake
of Demerol. Next week,
you will restring your guitar
because we will make you.

1

Breath-estranged,
4 January 1986 –
at least he had eleven days
to rage and regret.
They loathed him enough
to sing him out only
with the clanging of
cathedral death bells –
how was that, I wonder?

2

After six days you play
heavy metal loud through the night
and we, charged awake,
celebrate. At dawn,
you say my eggs
are like snot, swearing
as someone still alive.
Flushing your Demerol,
I shower-gasp away
the trailing blood
of night-shudder

as behind the bathroom door
you sing, sing to us
in a roaring joy
rib-full of
howling life-burst:
the boys are back in town.
And yes.
You are half right.

from Greenacre Park, Scunthorpe

Standing on graffiti swings, arcing high over
the new M181, we sniffed at rust on our fingers; squinted
down over the low, tiled roofs of Leys Estate
and the ditch on Holme Lane where murdered May Lovecroft
rotted, to the allotment where Mr. Mardsen
kicked me for treasure hunting in his cabbages,
beyond to the Co-op with its pyramids of treacle sponge,
and past the riverbank where Carrie Weatherlog conceived
the morning after seeing Little Angels play Wembley,
to the motorway, unravelling the world like a concrete carpet.
David Hilton said: if I told you to lick my boots
would you do it? He raised eyes to mottled skies
while Mandy Jones reached tongue to Doc Martens
and we were locked together in a swearing of disgust.

Some, like my father, whittle away slow rocking-horse days.
He polishes the altar of his Daimler running T-Cut over soft cream
like a lover's caress. She is meant for pub-lunch Sundays
not a motorway escape. In his garage, Don McLean sings about pie
in a country none of us knows. Mum is in the kitchen,
mixing Bird's Custard while we, in our tattered park,
launch futile dreams skyward. David Hilton will drop
one too many Falkland bombs and die alone,
a shake-head suicide. Mandy Jones will live long and love only him.
But for today, swings twist on squealing metal chains
somewhere high up on Greenacre Park
named for the farm now swallowed by sad streets.
We watch the M181 unravel like a grey future
while Dad polishes in slow curves, ever narrowing,
and Mum mourns her gravy in the park-green kitchen
where custard bubbles and a loud clock ticks.

a history

By three, it is almost night. Dense fog
windscreen-clings like a bogland boggart
as we wind along wet ribbon roads
beside the Wold, past the curtain droop of
sagging homes. The tarmac sweats, seeps sad tears
while rapeseed yellow-roars in sunset fields.

This was mine, once. A puttering descent
on teenage nights from the smashed-glass
roar and froth of steamy country pubs
to a smattering of rabbits, headlight-trapped
and twitching. I came from here. And here.

And here the place I strode out bold beneath a bus.
Here the mess of graveyard moss
where a bored priest stamped out his cigarette,
threw advice over too-hunched shoulders,
and left me in a drown of rain.

Here the hill where everybody died, still echoing
the long-drawn laughter of their last
life lust, the truck's honk-howling
as it gorged itself on dank monotony,
the road whipping like a wyvern's tongue.
Then: grief. I had already met the priest.

We should celebrate our frailties, he preached
at the funeral they shared. My frailty knew itself
on a final night: in a pound of footsteps,
a growl of hands too hairy, and a threat.
Two legs too few for running and next day
Up-stumble, stagger, pack, and go away.

ii.

winging it

Nine Toes (Waving and Drowning)

Last week, in Salzburg, I saw
a pickled, two-headed sheep
twisted fetal in a jar.
Yesterday, in Pitt-Rivers,
a desiccated dragon and the feet
of a mummy unravelling:
fork-spiked, end-shrivelled, black.
Today, while eating dill pickle,
I think about my tenth toe
floating in formaldehyde or
drying fig-like in the dark
corner of an incinerator.
No one said where they took it.

A small part of me mourned
by all the rest. Not big
as womb or kidney
nor small as foreskin.
Something in between
and stolen, like the right to walk
dark streets, head aloft
without fearing footfall.
On bad days I am baby,
fat feet flailing, bandaged,
and smiling in supposed wholeness
at white-coated cutters
who know one of my graves
though I do not.

On bad days
I have only nine toes
to wave at the world.

Travel Companion

The definition of "pelican" is a seagull
flying backward.
Here is an old man
who must fall asleep everywhere.
He neither mourns what has been lost
nor envies us.

We are visiting a stranger's house –
will see a picture of his nose
and the clippers
for the hairs in his nose.
At the ticket office, they tell me
he is a famous poet. Dead now.

Street signs here are shaped like fish.
I do not speak Spanish so
I do not know why they are shaped like fish.
On this beach, rocks grow black hair.
Sand holds shards of glass
and footprints that fizz and fade
with the tide.

The falling-asleep man
has hairs up his nose, like the poet.
Dozing in all the landscapes of the world
he has dreamed...
of dancing Cossacks, their boots on fire
oceans tickled pink by eel
castles pouring tar on tourists
a desert peopled by rain beetles.

Perhaps he dreams now of bald rocks and
fish swimming upstreet.
Sees himself flying backward
like the pelican.
His blurred footprints
speared by hourglass shards
collapse mournfully in sand.

in a Bad Mood (and loving it)

Everything is too wet here.
This bath, spilled soy milk,
sticky bubble stains, slick
saliva dribbling into ears,
and what's with the rain?

It wasn't wet in Merida.
Swimming pools shimmered
like hot air, white wine dried
on these lips and pale cheeks
pressed together, puffed up
fat as meringue.

It's too cold here. And pink.
And present. Too not-Merida.
And so draining. How
one day follows another
like a stalker. So what
if I melted the alarm clock.
We argued, which is kind of funny

and also sad. Sad, too, how the orderly
cars beyond this bath-steamed
window inch through rush-hour rain
not jostling one another –
not even putting up a fight:

what's with that? and the
swaying woman across
the street who pauses
to admire a wall –
how no one thinks to envy her.

For once, I'd like to be
on the backside of an
escalator just to see what
those marching stairs
become in a whispered
upside-down dark

or beneath a street lamp as
it drizzles one a.m., to see where
spilled light goes when
it dissolves in yellow water

or in an under-covers dark,
flashlight funnelled, with a
book I'm not supposed to read:
oh wait, there are no longer
books I'm not supposed to read

or please
just back in Merida.

Sleepless in Sanity I

This is an elegy to sleep.
From midnight, and a sliding through silver
when trees made love to the moon
then dropped it, merciless, in water
to squawking dawn and a light reprieve
there is a whirling of head-words
a not-quite-dreaming gentle ghost
of the floating fabulous:
blood dripping from needle thorns
tantalizing tarantulas, bleached
blur of an Inca mythology,
ten-foot-tall impenetrable rock
between furred light and bird flight
hawks plummeting on hares
the spine snap of wire trap
a calling through brambles
sliding down, mud side, hill-wise
to an ancient, rabbit-killer grove.
The soft implosion of toe-ripples
and beyond dream-memory
an ever-present creeping of words
gunshot sharp and spiralling –
a whorling life-rich near-death.
This is a no-sleep place.
Dog-howl transformed into night blur.
Otherwise, I welcome madness
in this mist of swimming foxes,
in this crisp light where time stops.
Grieve sleep. Fight panic.
Grow calm as dawn gathers
and stride out to meet the day.

Rhodes

On this table between four hands
so much head-clutter: a clotted
blood-sliver of roasted pepper

flesh shreds of salad onion
frigid, white-fat fries and
crumbs of feta: fragments

sliced from a plasticized brain.
These, the battle-scar remnants
of our morning after. This, the

death-debris of a head-spin
conversation: veined cabbage
skin, beer mats shredded, a curl

of fingers ice-locked into themselves.
After the pain-passing of gall-stone
olive pits, you spit. Grimace. Hate

hard stones in a soft mouth. Then
a hand – yours, or mine – reaches
across, convulsive, compulsive,

meets a jellied eel air thickness and
sobs back to itself. You sweep
our table clear with the forbidden

palm of a hand and we start again.
Later, we ice-slide a black harbour,
our gloves eel-skin thick, jammed

around hands, crammed into pointless
pockets. Our legs limp lettuce under
a bleached sky oozing ouzo, on the rocks.

Tail lights slice an artist's blood trail
in the sidewalk's skin when we stop
and you kiss my eye. Peel back lids

with your tongue, ease up and out
with a surgeon's lovely hand. This is
what it is to be devoured. An olive-black

pupil, slow-sucked in a warm mouth.
With a spitting of stones. Months from now

you'll miser away your jars of hoarded pits
like the dark souls of spent stars, taking
only a gloved left hand as a souvenir.

Whales. Volcanoes.

Never having seen
whales or volcanoes
I did not think they would exist.
In Costa Rica, a man
with hands like pistols
drew in mist
the outline of an absent cone.
Shrugged, squinted,
pitied us our lost wonder.
We saw only fish, finning through
shifting light.
In New Zealand, a man with bug eyes
scanned seas beyond the small boat's
tip and sway, finding only
eruptions of sea spume, sparkling.
Sky-spitting a white fire.
But now here
in this chalet in a red desert
something is parting.
Call it a fog, a dark,
a disbelief.
We saw those warnings,
corners curled and
taped to a wall:
in case of eruption, do not run.
Now something parts.
And there it is.
Conical and pushed up
into a knowing.
The biggest whale
the world has ever seen.

Aegean Mess

The forks here – real silver!
Do you feel the pitch and roll?
Since Saturday. Four times, he said.
Could someone pass the smoked salmon?
He's Turkish, you know. And very important.
Perhaps Odysseus sailed through here.
Your skirt – that pattern of barbed wire –
someone in the Secret Police, apparently.
The gold was cheaper, you know, in Rhodes.
His manners! And that outrageous moustache!
They moved her. The gay couple, he thought.
So sad. Did you try the brie and olives?
Offended her, yes. I cringed for them.
The Turkish Secret Police. How simply thrilling.
There's nothing to be afraid of, you know.
How do you train for a career in that?
Kusadasi, tomorrow, it's Tuesday.
Does anyone like halvah? baklava?
It was so blue, but you wouldn't want to swim in it.
They ship the carpets home, if you ask.
He looks so incongruous you'd never guess.
Girls ruin their eyes. The weaving blinds them.
My son's girlfriend is a model, but she had a face job.
Hence the expense. Carpets, value measured in eyes.
They made him walk through sewage, barefoot.
You have the perfect skin tone for rubies.
My linen never comes out this white at home.
Then they strapped him down to the chair.
The Secret Police? You don't say! He looks so sexy.
Pass the salt, could you? It's just a rumour.
We had our honeymoon in Istanbul.

Cattle prod to the fingers. Lips. It's true.
A good single malt makes everything right.
Ask if we can try the crème brûlée.
Or let's be brave! A platter of Turkish delight.

Judith

In the piazza by the one-armed woman
shaved from soft marble then sword-sliced,
he waits, watching the girl:
the one who drinks her coffee with
rice milk and has fine hairs on her two
arms that rise and prickle as she squints
into the middle distance, sensing.

He shrinks at a world all insides out
like the silk-skinned rabbit his father
once spread out on the table, teaching his
small son the beauty of art-death.

He has no idea where the lost arm went.
Truth is, with those only-marble muscles
she could not resist as the rapist-rope
of yesterday's defilers dragged her
to the mattress of this hard ground.

He knows all about Holofernes, how
the girl pushed back his head like
a lover before the plunge. There
was blood on her skirt as he died.

There are places for people like him,
his bare, beluga arms wrapped round
the flapping flesh of her future's
throat or wrestling with the raw and
skeletal bars of his own.

Yesterday, today, perhaps tomorrow
he will leave her untouched, but not so

next Tuesday, 5th June, at 2 p.m.
For now, her fine hairs sigh back
with relief at his little sacrifice. There
is a cliff he must jump from every day
and at the base, bones scattered
like trophies. He wonders if she dreams
of Artemisia: the fingers they sliced
to prove her rape as she scream-sank
in the nunnery of her mind's cell.

There is a smell of cooked meat
or burning books. Behind him,
the statue grows back her arm.
The girl wipes rice milk from her
lips, looks at the departing
curve of his back, fingers the blade
of a bright bread knife, and smiles
a private smile. She still hasn't noticed
the blood on her skirt.

to: Fernando Castro Pacheco

The Governor's Palace, Merida, Yucatán

You lunge for clarity in darkness, your light
refracted by the smoke of history:
Mayans, tough and cadaverous,
dreamed of by the yellow corn,
upheld by leaves of maize and
in the final panel, enslaved by sisal.

Translation is poetry but not all words
translate. Only art translates in callused hands,
whiplashed skin, and bloodied earth.
Forget corn. Forget sisal. Forget the Truth Cross.
These conquerors saw nothing
but by the brightness of a tortured dream.

See here: it could be stars you painted,
or drops of silence. Whiteness
is the blood of the light,
pouring down on a cosmos
where men speak strange tongues.
In the exiled jaguar of his rage,
someone made the great stones sing
before fading to an atheistic twilight
under the rutting flames
of a fevered, dying sun.

Three-Legged in Lima

In this fractured land, dogs have four legs
the same way cats have nine lives.
Legs are spent liberally here.

The mind of the poet paddles through
a pool filled with the feces of insects
though the water is gulp-pure.

Birds sleep by day, squabble by night
fighting with doghowl, gunshot, rabbitscream
under sleeping windows framed by a snore.

Here there are hills, moons, hours, poems –
all unclimbable: a bleached skull,
worm-riddled where the red wine grows.

Swimming through blurred words, elastic days
of pisco sour, pelicula, permiso – conversation
is a sonnet sung to mist before midnight.

Under the murderous grey of never-setting skies,
a crypt of bones, priest-sculpted into suns
and a condor feather, deftly snapped in two.

A pony grows from the dust of near-dark
swimming through felled stars, stunned –
snorting panic – life-lusting as a three-legged dog.

Sleepless in Sanity II

Is this intended?
A plunging back into
tight grasping onto
palms flat against
four shoulders of heartbeat
a South American safari
leaping down dirt tracks
on a truck's back.
Running out in front of us
a dream of giraffes.
Plane suspended overhead
praying for the plunge.

There came a gentler, mother-giving of advice.
Drink. Don't drink. Count. Sheep or metaphors?
Fear of stillness, silence, gathering madness.
It is the third night and there is panic.
Don't even think about it, one song
and a drink, then sleep must come.

A silent shivering. Six bodies now,
swimming the moon upstream.
Shards of ice star: shared shudders.
Broken glasses bobbing like message bottles.
A gasping at
gulping of
grasping at...
sharp memories
moon mythologized
a letting-go of seconds
and alone-fear.
Slipping down to a prayer.

There was a gentle tearing of awake-dream.
Walk through the dark night's half-open door.
At six, a flicker of word-mirage:
life is a liberation of torn butterfly wings.
Story fragments fizz and dissolve.
Lie still beneath the dozing,
like a face under water.
Try not to resist.
One song replayed
a hundred times
and sleep came.
Hallelujah.

Glastonbury

Slow dawn, picking through the debris of a spent night.
Whirling dancers wear the grass threadbare.
I am a headache, throbbing reckless abandon –
see their sandals and silks, tilting stilts made of crutches –

dancers whirling wear the grass threadbare,
feathers and glitter merge with mud and sweat.
Sandals and silks, tilting stilts made of crutches –
pungent dreams: this is my hallucination.

Feathers and glitter merge with mud and sweat.
Tents collapse with the weight of too much wild.
Pungent, dreamed, I am hallucination;
fires across fields; soft pockets of silence.

Collapsed tents, tumble-weighted by wild.
I am my headache, throbbing reckless abandon.
Fires across fields, soft pockets of silent stars.
Slow dawn, picking through the debris of a spent night.

Home

"...a joyous shot at how things ought to be"
– Philip Larkin

You, like this bay, are a thumbprint soft-pressed
between crumbling cliffs, tide-washed with sadness,
knowing that tomorrow we go home.

Your hermit crabs spin ever-widening circles in their
plastic bucket. They do not exchange their shells, only
joy-dance the endless walls of their plastic heaven.

As the waves recede so do you, beneath sloping streets
soft-sliding seaward. Though you leave the rocks behind
you take with you the imprint of barnacles on your thighs.

Today, you are a little more lost in the torn rag of each
lone seagull's cry. You say you lack poetry, yet the bruise-black
of your eyeliner seeps farther down your cheek each day.

You had a kitten until the night before you left. They told you
he went to a farm so he could be happy forever. From the way
you say "farm," it's obvious you know what this means. And the way

you stare back at the solid stone of the fisher-cottages:
people living there for decades went unremembered. What
hope is there for you? Today's tide beckoned and when you

did not surrender, tore its seaweed to tatters. Sharp rocks
shook their unshorn heads at goodbye clouds meagre as an
orphan's slop-porridge. Now, even the rock pools are empty.

Only at the airport, when they ask for your address, will you
crumple, recalling the sea and how it wanted you. The comfort
of cliffs cutting through water and old cottages caught between

the embrace of centuries and the skeletons bricked in their
walls. Oblivion, like the cold-grey waves, is welcome when
nothing else is left but the long, slow run into the sea.

iii.

fewmets and flames

Lady, not Lazarus

after Sylvia Plath

The third time,
my thirty-year-old dear,
you could not do it.
You triumph in failure,
perhaps.

Your blood is a cranberry-bright
salute to the dodo's doom
and a two-thumbs-down
to the fat gold watch
of your babies'
brief life-lust.

You spoke it like
debridement: a surgical
easing off of dead skin
to the feel-alive agony of
ripe flesh peeling.

Franken-shocked, your rebirth
happened but twice, my dead dear
(not once for the copycats, though,
nor the puzzling fight and fire
of death-hover's
sudden life desire).

Thinking to shuffle in
the fourth of nine lives
did you expect
a coming back, sheepishly,

to the dawn of your infants'
mute and disapproving gaze?
Welcome, instead, to
eternity's cloven pine.

Dying is pure theatre;
a rehearsed and Plath-played part
now settling in for the extended run.

We bought you piece by piece:
hair, eyes, your heart,
the knee,
the price twice-charged,
post-tragedy.

And Hughes?
After life's ash-heat,
let fall those
leaves of raw regret
on one who would not forget.

Here, your victory.

Whiteout

There was one snowflake last Sunday
unlike any other
as you sat in your white car
(the engine running)
and pretended you did not exist.

The snowflake fell with a thud,
hit the deep slush-rut in the December road
made by your persistent tires,
joined a sad procession of thawed snow
plodding in top hats and black skirts
toward the dark gutter,
and slid into oblivion.

By morning, snow was only a memory
though nothing else had thawed.
A wind-whipped limb
amputated from the age-old apple tree
fell across my garden path
and I was tempted
on the eve of a new day
to read it as a sign.

Perhaps I only thought you were there,
your car looking furtively
back over its shoulder
as spring came and it melted
like the frosted figures
on a too-tiered wedding cake
placed next to a fake log fire.

forward moving back

We make our way along this painted line:
seagulls landing belly-first on water
like jets with broken wheels; fractured
tortoises struggling onward
merely because others insist.
Years are so slight. We are
smaller than a child's lunch box.
Without hope or possibility,
our flesh dissolves.
Experiment with us. Once lured into water,
we forget how to swim as the lengths
lope steadily into next year.
We loiter amid moving cars,
unable to give up a lifetime's ritual,
still as a rat's gruesome gaze and
glinting in a single glass eye. At the end,
we find ourselves herded into enclosures,
tumbled down stone steps and upended
like foul creatures spun too long by the tail.

Like foul creatures spun too long by the tail,
tumbled down stone steps and upended,
we find ourselves herded into enclosures,
glinting in a single glass eye. At the end,
still as a rat's gruesome gaze and
unable to give up a lifetime's ritual,
we loiter amid moving cars,
lope steadily into next year.
We forget how to swim as the lengths
experiment with us. Once lured into water,
our flesh dissolves.
Without hope or possibility,

smaller than a child's lunch box,
years are so slight. We are
(merely because others insist)
tortoises struggling onward
like jets with broken wheels. Fractured.
Seagulls landing belly-first on water,
we make our way along this painted line.

Confronting an Island

My four o'clock is late, riding the ferry
from an island shoot. Ducks, here,
on a lake that should be frozen:

mergansers, awkward with loon-envy,
spinning gravy circles, gravely, beyond
a place where blades slice into rink

below a place where skater legs belong.
An emptiness of ticket booth, an emptiness
of boardwalk, an emptiness of

always talking over cold fries, cold
fires, curled sheet music, crumpled files,
and burned coffee always, talking over.

These ducks, not squabbling today, trace,
in this absence of squabble, of sound,
silver music in bright sun-circles,

this world a split-bottomed marble bag
an absence of ice on a lake, a no one
of people, some of them hurting us

round the Power Plant: please use other
door use other door use other – an endless
exclusion; if time is money, I am losing

my mind, crouching low to the water, peering
up through a buckled, winter-bleached bush
to obliterate this wept city:

someone unseen is drilling, my teeth
set against chatter, where torn flags flap
by the envy-eyes of ducks, watching,

and here, in this watch-stopped time,
I wait for you like a decoy, for a wiping
out of islands, an outlawing of loonshoot,

tossing boredom to the dip-sink of duck
heads, like hope, through water that
does not stop-freeze birds, or a ferry.

at a standstill

In sunshine, thousands running for the cure:
teens sweating into cells, snarled in ribbon,
celebrating mothers, dead, as the band sings:
don't worry! be happy! Inside the glass
cowboy hat, in the atrium's atheist church,
a silent roadrunner plays on a twenty-foot screen.
Children yell: that's not a good idea! – as the
pneumatic drill digs a hole large enough for
teens to fall into. No one can scream
with the sound turned down. This morning,
thousands of Afghani women dressed
their daughters up as sons: a burst of freedom,
a race against budding breasts. There is no
dignity, no sanity in obsession. Only fatalism.
A tomorrow sadness. Ask coyotes.
At the birth of twin girls, they told her
to put aside exhaustion and mourn.
While the roadrunner disappears in a
puff of dust, Wile E. Coyote finds herself
leaping off a cliff; is suspended in the
child-hope of possible flight, before the fall.
It replays. And replays. Again she dies,
which is why we run for the women
in our lives until the band stops, the screen
slips to black, and a small voice says,
"That's all, folks."

after

More than these swans
muted, today.
This river, a moss-sunk
sloth, the salmon
constantly at their
jump and fail
cardinals bleached
robin-dull and those
sky-swimming seagulls
paper-cutting their
newspaper clouds.

A day that rushed
now seeps and pools.
Only the leaden leaves
thud groundward.
Everything is stripped
of something: this bench
of its paint, my coat
of its lining, this
morning of meaning,
even this poem
left bare, not knowing
where it meant to go.

woman, a wind

wind is rising
and a moment before was not like this:
each raindrop a fragment of dry leaf
each cloud a murky lake stirred –
how sudden
                    you say
voice galloping on invisible feet
leaving an absence of nothing

her cigarette, a butterfly now
your untouched beer a tsunami, the road
a swirling mess of horse drownings
below windows, throwing people from them
blisters burned to this hand popping
like fireworks, and on her table pistachio shells
tap dancing, and under the table
a child-part of someone, ball-rolled
cloud-chewing, spitting out dry leaf

each street sign a cricket bat
each cricket bat a canoe paddle
each canoe paddle a microphone stand
and Frank Sinatra singing "All of Me"
into a mic from a passing canoe
wearing cricket whites and chewing
on my cigarette's dead wings

risen wind is falling now
and I drink my beer, crack pistachios
under sudden sun
watching the thin, smoking woman
on this plastic patio chair
set fire to fingers, her skin rising
to fall childwards in a dry leaf rain

Threads

"Threads was aired in 1984 before an unsuspecting UK TV audience... then quietly removed...until 2002."
– YouTube comment

Teacher says: only working-class children
short on brains and sophistication
would giggle at the little people
running backwards. He sniffs at us
and fingers his silk dicky bow as the video
rewinds. Still, we can't help laughing
as cars land safely the right way up,
limbs regenerate, darkness spins to a twilit hope,
mushroom cloud fizzles to a spore.

Kill the lights, Crawley
and Crawley
kills the lights

The Soviet Union has moved warheads into Northern Iran.
There's still time for a few pints! At noon the US ultimatum expires.
There is no cause for alarm. The public is urged to remain
calm. *Nowt we can do about it, we might as well enjoy ourselves!*
Hospitals have been cleared for expected casualties. This is just
a precaution. *The noise on't streets is nobbut the pubs turnin' out.*
Known and potential subversives have been arrested. There's no
reason for concern. If someone dies in your fallout room, label
the body with their name.

the video blinks black and
Crawley hits the lights

See, children, Teacher says,
we are all of us as powerless as you.
Little people, running aimless in a fast dark or
blinking in a sudden blind of light:
what's the difference?

The squeaking swings we smoke our fags on
and the local where our daddies drink
and the bingo hall, the Mothercare,
the Bookies, British Homes Stores,
pikelets, pints and pinafores
teacakes, fairy cakes, fish cakes
space invaders, trident missiles,
the placards on Greenham Common,
everything melting to a mess,
our flesh a glue to hold it fast, fires
burning, fingers burning, all our lives
burning. There is a frantic something
in Teacher's voice: he knows he done wrong
to make us watch it, he done wrong
and now the working-class children
without brains sit in their own
non-giggling twilights, replaying
those cars flying skyward
and a mushroom cloud blooming
as the whole world waits
for the end to begin.

Cat, Coffee, You

after Mark Strand

Each day I feed the cat
and pull the string to
play with the cat and
stroke the cat.
All days, until one day
the cat dies.
There is no cat, and
then again there is
no cat and in between
for fifteen years
there is cat.

Each morning I fill
the coffee maker
with four scoops of
Ethiopian Yrgacheff –
and press the switch
and then remember
to plug it in and
there is no coffee
then there is coffee
and in between
just a faint hiss
like an exhalation.

At Gare du Nord
I am waiting for you.
There is no you
and then there is you.

There is train and no train
and there you are:
a moment in time
waiting for the empty air to fill.
A saying of goodbye
even as you walk
toward me. You are not
here and again not
here and in the small crack
between denials you are
brief anticipation
and lost.

Dread and Fishes

In the bleached rock pool
of today's November garden
small stones hold firm like barnacles,
soaked trees weave their impossible fronds,
and frost-wilted plants waver
in the cloying waters
of a fog-thickened air. An unknown cat
slinks fishlike through the murk.

It is difficult to breathe
in this endless waiting-to-surface,
seaweed-stranded in dank half-life,
our amniotic not-life, this
rot of a how-to-survive life.
Everyone does it better than I,
not seeming to notice or care
when clouds erupt like bubbles
or the sun squints with its one
all-seeing eye like a child
leaning too far over a bridge
and destined to fall.

Night descends like poured oil
and we mark the time to
a plunge-float up to
the gasping surface, stilled
and perhaps belly-up, carrying
the forgotten mystery of what
lies below and harpooned, no doubt,
by sharp disappointment.

Rising may be falling, after all,
the sun no eye but a burning hellfire
to tip to and the suck and pull
of that small black cloud nothing
but a single-celled rock pool
awaiting one more caught and
floundering fish.

There are worse places
than here, we think,
looking up to a comet tail
shaped exactly like a seagull's beak.

Coma Toes

the definition of friendship
is one thin sliver through a
life – door held ajar
for a slipping in –
a silver-lined shadow
easing through, sideways

on Everest sits a lone girl
with turned-black toes. Her voice,
muffled by the vulture wings
of a flapping tent and splintered
by an ice-hot wind
cries against an amputation of lips

the beach is empty but for an old man
dozing by the flaked paint
of his father's Punch and Judy stage
his puppets limp beside
arthritic hands too stiff
to take on lives like a glove

miles above our laughter, a child curls
into his wordless fear of flight,
and his torso, sucked suddenly
through the airline window,
stretches into bat-flapping
strands of night

something from the mind
slips out on a tongue
we call this words not spoken
and sometimes
the lost hope of a song

a morning

how the eyelid
peels back
disbelieving

here is day
beyond bedsheets
wearing hands
like gloves

sneak up
on a mirror
to find a face in it

wall folded
into stairs now
for a walking
down

carpet still here
dead houseplant
here rusted
kettle here

from taps: water
it does not
dissolve skin

tear back eyelids
from windows
today
there is
world

Cooking Solo

Tonight, a soufflé – talc-soft, finger-white: coaxed into being by these eyes, blinking in an oven door.

Tomorrow, a must-not-burn macaroni, first stovetop then cheese bubble-crusting under broiler, blistering black as a timer screams.

On Saturday, the hot-breath hope of chicken pie, pastry crust wing-flapping a bowl-dashed desperation as it cooks itself to death.

Outside these dark windows, the street runs like ice cream. Trees birth black needles to burst star-holes in a wet sky. Someone unreachable glances over at my house through knife blades of inedible grass. It is blister-hot in here now, the oven door open to a smell of cremations.

I am writing you that letter.

iv.
dragon dance

Reeling in a Child

I tried under Fly Fishing, Cooked
Fish, Fishing Holidays, Fish
Breeding, Fish Eye Lenses,
One Fish, Two Fish in Picture Books
and the DVD section: Nature.

Many people were you from behind.
No one was you from the front.

Then, sadly, I tried Lost & Found,
asked: have you seen a child
about, oh, yea high –
looks like everyone from behind
only herself from the front
you will know her by the trailing red twine,
by the obvious absence of
all other. No luck.

Next, I tried Japanese trawlers
off the Grand Bank, reeling in
caplan by the wasted millions
but no you. Tried looking
in gaiters anchored in the
Okanagan River, and searched
between the blood-bites
of piranhas, down the Amazon.
Finally I got clever: tried gossip
columns for fishing of a different
sort and the League for the Prevention
of Cruelty to Fish in case
this fish thing was an unkind joke.

Over the years, I've tried
the flake-pink innards of salmon,
seaside aquariums, even the rib cage
of a baleen whale before I remembered:
a whale is not a fish.

Today, you turn 90 and I am starting
to believe you will not come. Perhaps
you went fishing instead. I will wait
until you turn 101, then toss away this bucket
of aging minnows I call bait, grieve,
and take up salsa. Following daughter-hints
somewhere between a whisper and a dream,
I will wait for you in the section
marked "Dance" as a couple
dozen years squeeze by.
Hang on. Did you mean the dip?

Brother

Sleepless, she spoons grinds
in a grey kitchen beneath
the snow-stuffed chimneys' choking
mouths. There are holes in the walls
and she peers into the sleep of others.
There are holes in the floor
and she peers into a sacred burial.
The coffee mug goes
walking in the night
and she follows the clattering chatter
of spoon-stirred thoughts
through snow-sodden streets
to the place where it began.

He is not chest-crushed
but waits, a white-haired toddler
for more than fifty years. She passes him
coffee, which he cups between tiny,
arthritic hands, and they stand
together in shoulder-touching sadness
while coffee spoons
polka-spin to a silent song.
He will flinch at motorcycles
as he should have back then
and nudge her night through
its mind-numbed, caffeine maze.
There is a squeaking swing
at the end of the world;
screaming neighbours,
surgeon saws, frying pans flying,
garden gates standing too open,
and the irreverent singing

of colour-fed canaries.
There are lilies
on a coffin small enough
to hold aloft with one hand.
The coffee seeps up an arm,
neck-buzzes her,
washing eyeballs
in grit-sludge,
and she spins forward
through a sugar swirl
of high streets, weeping
for those fifty years.
She sad-smiles back at tiny,
transparent arms like twigs sunk
in hoar frost, bites down
on coffee grinds,
and sleeps.

receiver

a heavy phone call came along
it made our phone ring
it made our goldfish jump
and the fuchsia paint
painstakingly chosen
for her room
melt from the walls
wriggle back into the can
and slam down the lid

stiff fingered, receiver in hands
we wait for news
of sudden life
spewing over like lava
but expect, instead
rattling telemarketers
a great aunt gossiping
a parrot accusing Winston
Churchill of murder –
all scenarios more likely:
we wait, and listen

and afterwards, stare in
a mirror at wrinkled cheeks
unfurling like buds
see beyond our reflection
a sun move backwards
through a sky

down in the street, a boy
blows bubbles
sucks bubbles   inflates

and blossom-rises to the
arms of a tree

we are elated by the
soon-to-be-news
in twenty-four hours it
will be yesterday
but first a telephone
must ring and this time
it does not matter
if we choose to answer

Chinese Character

Before we knew your character,
little lone one, daughter –
you were a rebel, a dog's bark,
insurgent, as in Falun Gong:
a negative, a not-to-be, disused,
blossom soft as a town in spring,
a rapid thing, something buoyed
by the air. You held within your
name a rejection, but then
you were also a kind of radish.
Trifling, meagre, even baggy.
Luxuriant as lungs knowing how
to dispel, drive away, disobey –
oh, little ten-curled-toes,
what joys in store.

Then we saw your character
in ink ribbons still birth-wet
from the artist's brush, and she said,
interpreting tones and swirls:
Fei is very nice, smelling of
flowers. Chinese use it for a
girl name that mean pretty
and beautiful. She is fragrant
flowers in the most modest
and polite way, this waiting one.

All good. But we know. On
even days, she will be a radish.
On Mondays, a dog's bark.
On the third of the month,
luxuriant as lungs. In spring,

a rebel. In adolescence, a
negative, a rejection. And
only always, in secret places,
a flower, delicate, fragrant
with self.

Strange Thing

Cradled in your stork-white envelope
you are something beautiful,
and here, a strange thing:
one week ago I was a not-mother;
no child, no girl, no baby
in the world had a claim on me –
then, because a man who has a
chipboard cubicle, acne, three cats,
dental phobia, ten chess boards
and a view over the Forbidden City
willed it
this became not-true
and in a land without my language
that has never felt the touch of my feet,
he pasted my life onto yours
before breaking for chrysanthemum tea
or to call his lover in a secret place
or to speak with a psychotherapist
about that dental phobia.
So now I am mother.
Please forgive me – I do not know you
or your name, the smell of your
breath or the press of a cheek or the
cry you make when an ear aches,
but you –
my strange, my unknown thing –
will lose your homeland soon
and wipe out me,
the not-mother. In the hold
of a plane you wing
toward me in your stork-white
envelope, a too-pink photograph

shock-blinking in sudden freedom
from a prison crib, something
too perplexing, too unknown yet,
too much the stranger these
next and long two months,
to be who you may one day be –
my something beautiful.

Waiting One

We met you for the first time
in a pink-frosted photograph,
Ronnie McDonald growing
out of your head: your
quizzical expression, bars
still hanging before your eyes,
our future hanging there too –

people's reactions: your grandfather says,
"I'll make a start on the rocking horse,"
and a neighbour: "She was born five days
and fifty-six years after me, so we can party together!"
and a six-year-old cousin: "Is China on a cloud?" Your
great-grandmother: "I had a heart fixed today," and
my father-in-law: "I hid champagne in your sofa."
A friend with cancer: "She is the only good news
I've had all year," and finally, me to your dad:
"Our unknown daughter is half the length of this rug."

I must leave you now, as I often will,
for a moment or two, to gestate a second
self, but know this: on 28 February 2006
as you slept behind the bars of your
Ronald McDonald room,
half a google earth away, in a city
of a million bicycles,
where the principle exports
are copper, zinc:
you entered our lives.

Overwhelm

In the cracks between this joy
worlds crumble.

She sobs, holding her
swollen belly, clasping
tight those acrobat legs,
"I'm spotting, and the only
trapeze for me now, the
desperate upside down –
an against-gravity
squeeze-fetus
futility."

He says, today she turns
thirteen and sobs into his
thirteenth beer, remembering
how the two-year-old loved
hats, the six-year-old
chess, the nine-year-old
flared jeans and
the twelve-year-old
turning her back
on a father.

In the canyon of these
crumbling worlds she
sits, her photograph
a throne, thumbsucking
our guilty pleasure
as we emotion-heave
a single pierce
of light.

between falling

after Lisa Jarnot

between falling in love
a spore print of mushrooms
crisped centipedes in a basement
small fires and soup-thick sleep

between falling in love
fingers wiggle when I tell them to
mind terror-snaps open during surgery
a sparrow dies by a kettle, boiled dry

between falling in love
slipping into panic, never conscious,
as cognac dribbles down a chin,
that you are also slipping toward –

between falling in love
is a hard clutching of too-smooth bars
in a darkness seeping tears,
and outside that holding cell, nothing

between falling in love there is
birth there is death and
there is now, which is neither, and
each state masquerades as another

Leap Forward

On crumbled walls
red paint of Mao
screaming now
where Lao Tsu
whispered
eternity.

Let us tear the world
to pieces,
you and I.

Jade could be
more green, peach
more luscious,

the air not so
acrid with
dead panda
putrefaction.

Paint me a lake
bobbing with
not-so-lucky fish

or sing me a
mountain
hollow-eyed and
shorn.

Not a boot in
the face, all this,
nor revolution,

but a glorious bonfire
of books.
Say we did it
in the name
of culture:

for the poetry
of our future
we give you
a past to mourn.

T Minus One Hour

Today, in our ever-morning:
sky the colour of hard cheese
stamped with the chicken-slow
of pterodactyl winging over the
residue of a gone life, like the
clatter of corroded army medals
in a metal box. Tick-tock has broken
free of its clock and seasons a
sneezing sky. See below: armbands
of aging communists spread on the grey
bread of your river because there is
a coup in progress somewhere in
an elsewhere that has an evening in it,
and is not here.

Needle nerves I am, by this window,
bending over someone else's
view, watching the day print
itself on the hotel's complimentary
soapbox, upended for these
feet to stand on, floating like a
life raft through the fluid-blackened
lungs of the Pearl Delta.

Push-pin me down in Guangzhou
here on the cracked map's laminate,
so you may tell me where I am or
who I may be soon in this flipped coin
of a newborn day, then tell her my
river is a passage that is not the passage
of time. No one has escaped a place
as time-locked as it is landlocked,

nor do the neon bright of lying
boats hide the truth of effluence
flowing beneath affluence. Do not
think we will leave behind this
Pearl, little waiting one. It will
flow beneath us as we paddle you
to a future where the Yangtze River
Dolphin is no more. I will hold
you above it, but never be quite
good enough to cancel out its stink.
Someone is calling us now.

Flagship

In this light
see baby,
biceps bulging.
Planting
your body-flag
in rage you
spread-eagle,
saying: I claim
this much.

Eel-slipped
from your mother
as that mother
eel-slipped
from you.
My cuckoo now,

wearing your
two names
like a double
whammy
as you
swim in
the too-big
skin of both.

You guard
your self
like a
time-locked
secret, sailing
your ship

toward
a future
unknown
while I
riding
the storm

follow

before the fall

Thirty flights above the Pearl River
and five feet from us, two window cleaners
rope-dangle their fate. It is windy today
as a jet engine howling, and hot.
The men's wives pray so hard for no wind
they sway like three-inch golden lilies.
And here, big-footed, bath-soft, and sleep-swathed,
we press noses to the safety of glass, hotel pickled
in the stale air, and watch. Baby bottom
squashed into the crook of this arm. Fat fists
window-flattened. Milk mouth open
to blow them kisses, or a wind. How safe
it is here for her, in these arms, swaying,
and how not-safe for them, in the arms
of their wind. We wait as the slick river
oil-eel slithers by in wet tar silver
like a slowly forming net and we know
there is fear, for why else dangle in twos?
This pair, daily making a kind of love:
one is a pendulum, but two, the hopeful hands
of a clock. We, too insulated to hear
their ticking as they ponder in a wind
between here and not here. Between torn-wing
insects and an epic Daedalus. Baby fingers
push through glass like water as the frantic
fingers of these life-dangling men
out-clutch for each other in a fear shared
only by their daughters, sleeping at home
in cribs three feet too far from the ground.

The Forbidding City

Enter the inner sanctum of the
ancient Chinese Character
backwards, through the Gate of
Heavenly Peace. Rest awhile in the
House of Yearbound Delight before
Walking Upright through the Terrace
of Five Colour Earth, aiming for
Prosperous Harmony and Enhanced
Righteousness. On your long journey
to the Gate of Character Cultivation,
join the human push and pulse for the
garden of Kindliness and Tranquility;
the Palace of Peace and Longevity.

You may find the search for
inner exactitude too forbidding:
in which case, follow the forward
pull, the great leap, the strong
march through the wasteland,
and into the comfort of the first circle
of hutong-Hell. Here, long-bearded
smiles rise out of smoke and stone.
A child with rotting legs and perfect
teeth is crocheting elephants and
eternal love meets sudden squeal of
pneumatic drill, facing obliteration.
Soon, Character Cultivation will be
the only choice in the Great March
Forward and more will wither in a
future replete with Enhanced
Righteousness than the two tree stumps
of a small girl's gangrenous feet.

Four-Legged in China

To shout an insult here is to sing in perfect pitch
drowned by a scream-chorus of diggers
cracking open the world. A single act of

carelessness means eternal loss of beauty
reads Confucius, in loco parentis, above
the flopping-fish girl with the barbecued feet.

Our Beijing is a bomb blast in brush-painted
beauty, sky stained sepia where no birds fly
(not even forward) and Gobi Desert dust,

long-bearded, smiles: funnelling from smoke
and stone. The price of chopsticks? Forty
thousand trees a year, says the man who races

crickets, razing hillsides where once
the poetry of peonies grew. Now, this tiny hai zi
legs-dangles me like a Li Po moon, lantern-

swaying her arc-song; black fumes of jet hair
rising, fat fists unfurling to wave
at our world, small head self-crammed

new-hatched from three cracked lives. Silk swathed.
Glorious. Joining her two legs to mine.
Replete with her ten-toed perfection.

infancy

Mornings, now: baby-stagnant. Outside these windows, beyond the sob and yawn of a barred crib fist-clutched, light the colour of sour milk leaks through lavender. In here, small fingers grip 5 a.m. around the throat of my thumb. And morning will bleed into a slow solo walk through streets changed, where the puddles of yesterday cat-curl, surly, and seep along curbs, and the rushing-by of briefcase-dangling suits is as alien as in before-baby but now in a fresher, eye-blinking way. My alone-noon will be a thrilling in solitary stillness though an umbilical cord of never-break pulls back to a cold crib in a dark room where sudden child hovers.

There was a never knowing, until today: the sound of sunshine nor the way the road is feather-stroked by cars nor the way the body rocks to soothe both child and self, in the absence of. There was a never knowing; a world replete with life and the two sides of hope in all its infancy.

Until today.

Nor Can Foot Feel, Being Shod

Do you, like the old woman,
live here in my shoe, scraping
dead matter from between toes,
swinging apelike on a frayed
boot lace? Today, the shoe
has mile-high springs, tomorrow
blades that clash and by next
week, ten-inch nails and a vise.

Slide your fingers over this heel
like a satin slipper and follow
with a tongue. We were taught
feet are for running through
poppies. Shoes were born of a
first upright standing and now this
baby flails a puppet-flop of fat
feet while her mother ties on
pink booties with hairy fingers
and a scratch of underarm.

Back then, we slipped feet onto
paduka platforms, mincing paths
between microbes; tight-roping cracks;
god-plucking bugs from certain death.
Shedding shoes, we sank soles into
fruit, relishing grapesquelch. But this
was in a dreamtime, long ago.
I wore Doc Martens beneath
a wedding dress, little guessing
you wore steel-toe-capped boots.
Now my feet have chosen
shoes to wear when they die.

Today, kissed feet are crushed; toes
forced under arches, bent, broken,
bound: you say erotic. These bindings,
loosened in a sighing dark, weep
flesh. Mind pulsing a belly-swim
through poppies I will not tell her,
my Chinese lotus, my three-year
golden lily: your mothers share
a knowledge of this pain.

No Depth

Caplin and capuchins: that's all there is, for now.
Caplin swimming close to the surface
like jewelled dreams almost cupped in a hand.

And where's the monkey's eyes? There's the monkey's eyes!
Depth lost beneath a baby's giggle when there
is only a stone to suck, to ward off hunger.

Wailing babies, we waited under a mourning wind
on a promontory in the raging shipwreck of a
pre-spring storm and prayed for caplin in the

waves' swollen bellies and for the small, hopping
shrieks of children clutching caplin in their monkey fists
and for the soft sands all silvered over with fish

forced to these shores by the tide. Now we have our caplin
and our capuchins and, loving both with bellies full,
we still wonder at the lost promise of scarlet macaws and

the thrill of a poison dart frog, standing in the dying light
of a lost day with this monkey fist-clutching our heart,
and the emerald waste of fish scales sliding under our feet.

halved

I am talking on a telephone
to you, while you, lying
in a hospital bed,
talk to a girl
beside your bed
who is me.

What was that?
"Hold on. Hold the line.
This girl by my bed,
this girl who is also you,
is trying to speak."
I hear her cry out
my surprise, thinking
me the imposter, then
the sound of you,
softly laughing
at this something severed
as you tumble
into drugged sleep while
the live phone line
lies between two who
should be one and I
will always
wonder, will
always
wonder.

Ten years later when
I am lighter, wearing
one sock, leaving
for work a half-hour late, drinking

cider pints by halves, making
half-hearted attempts to
understand – you will
swear, still
swear
I was real
that day,
by your hospital bed,
as I talked
on the phone's
other end. You will say
this split half slipped
out on a shadow,
riding on the starched
hem of a nurse-skirt, say
you still grieve for that part
(yours as much as mine),
and we will know, both of us,
that this girl who left
me trailing in her wake,
is at least half
                        gone,
her arched body
flicking a death-smile
as our futures
gulp her.

Mudslide Memories

I have known this place before:
a summer camp slipped soft into mud
when a life rage of raw living
explodes brown bodies from camp cabins.
Instinct-led, feeding a feral joy-fear,
the children come, slapping towels
in circle squeals, roaring, racing,
slip-sliding in primal soup,
falling mud-backwards into slop,
slick-racing hillsides, pig-wallowing
in mud pucker, laughter blurring
the soft space between wild world
and this whirling wild. Memory is a
fat-arm-flailing, dark-future-defying,
hot summer day when mud
dam-bursts free
out of drought.

*

I have known this place before:
this veteran-dazed Vimy,
this patch of Canada in some forgotten field.
After millennial rains, in memory-trenches,
mud-mired children slide, a firing squad
of squeal-screams, trench feet flailing,
making dirt guns of brown fingers,
chasing a thrill-plunge beneath bomb-drop,
faces afire, cheeks flamed, mud-slipping into
the glory-death of grandfathers.
Veteran, watching, sees skin rot in
ten-year-old boots, sees in lonely headlock

a not-from-fingers bullet flying
a not-child voice of lost friend screaming.
For this, his almost-child chums died;
this magnificent trench-chasing of
bright futures unfurling. He captures
a darting child-soldier, holds his own
non-gun trigger-cocked in fingers
gnarled, then sticks it through
the thin crack of a shared smile,
and fires.

Vegas, again

Here, flamingoes have barely a leg to stand on
and the black space between each desperate neon
would be another loss of faith, if we still had it.
Seven years ago, it drained away: we dropped rage
at your absence as others dropped poker chips.
I wrote you a postcard right here, misery swelling
like a filled belly, and cried because there was
nowhere to send it. In the absence of baby,
we nursed the luxury of falling apart.

Tonight, dressed
in flamingo-pink
you wrecked our room
with your rolling
and bouncing
your fluffed flamingo
flouncing, mimicking
dolphin dance and
a white lion roar.
We knew, this time,
a different kind of faith.

It is difficult to detect the winds of change
among the whir of air conditioners,
yet once the ocotillo bloomed here, tatty
as a picked-over turkey, and what came after –
this well-heeled, high-heeled, hungering, opulent hell –
is only the result of an excessive pruning.
You are this city's opposite, little wild rose.
A messy grafting that grew into a tangle of ever-joy,
a Bellagio fountain of fizzing lights the night
the computer program malfunctioned

and delighted revellers celebrated
the dizzy wonder of random spray,
singing in tongues across a sidewalk light-flecked
as a desert, back when the ocotillo bloomed.
You teach the flowering desert's sad regret
that it is still possible for a flamingo to stand,
flashing its showgirl pink at a barren future
even when the final leg has been lost.

First September

There is a frost-soft
covering of light where
the nighttime walked
and, leaves rasping,
the trees whisper into day.

She cries her legs
to school, grief-stricken
and her tear shards
shatter the concrete.

I want to tell her what
I know: like leaves
we cannot turn
without falling.
Growth is the end
of fat knees slipped
into soft laps, a dazed
and sleep-deprived
peace, Queen Street
lattes and stroller wheels
puddle-churning all those
endless afternoons.

All that loss replaced
by this, my push, and
that, her stagger:
a brutality of bells and
lost-face five-year-olds
snaking off to their first
Monday morning
9 a.m.
war.

Signs of Decay

Deboning dragons or debunking myths:

that the stork ever stood coffin-still
on a birth-wet lawn at 2 a.m. pronouncing
it's a girl! 6 lbs 5 oz and healthy! both
mother and child are doing well!

or that this slow, revolving globe can't be,
at the same time, flat, despite the witch-
burning of a 2,000-year-old science –

that unattached six-year-olds won't float
clown-side down and round like a fetal self
beginning a seventy-year death choke
at the end of a stilled birth cord,

or that the yellowed teeth of each passing year
won't rewrite in crooked, marble gravestones
every tale they told us would be true,

or that we won't go there and back just to see
how far it is, for the hell of it, applying the
Tao of a rock climber to the raising of a child.

We devour the parasitic myths of our choosing,
not theirs, chewing on truths while they still leak
flavour, then spitting them out like gum. What

do I know? Only these warm hands in last night's
toothless dark, the silent despair of this never-sleeping
child, and the bath bubbles she calls her fairy friends,
popping like too-tall tales as the years lurch by.

Snow Suitor

Snow is running through subways
fast and slantwise as a train
clattering a rice-spill of flakes onto faces.
Under shivering tracks, small nests
of curdled milk for a lying-in
of mud-coloured mice. Snow
pools and arcs in the ticket seller's
eyes, bloodshot, and he cries
through the red ice of tears, though
his lips smile always. Today, snow runs
in his veins, gathering in the
dark corners of a secret heart,
clogging up a click-shunting muscle
and through the drift on drift
and snow on snow bursts
the arterial train, stopping. The man
who leaps down into heartstorm
is his lover, heel-dancing on the
soft red tissue of each beat,
trampolining through his passion
as on a thin sliver of too-fresh meat.
There is snow on the sleeves of his
jacket. Icicles dangle from his lobes.
These men: they watch each other from
inside the snow-whirl of a ticket seller's
heart, and the lover, quick-fading,
steps back into whiteout. The parent-heart
gives birth to a wild wind sigh.
His hand sells a ticket. His eyes swing
to a clock. He smiles, always and sadly.
His shift will end soon, with the storm.

Where to Begin

You'll never know if there are others
picking your route through this dark.

A lost boy: he knocks at number three,
waits, and shoulder-slumps to the next house
not yet desperate and perhaps
only canvassing, after all.

There is the woman who leaves
skin and blood on your roses,
thorned while corner-crossing,
who pain-smiles, wonders
what it means. Perhaps nothing.

Planting in the rain, your fingers
thrust onions to a suffocation,
noting how swiftly the little graves fill
with water. There is lurid fascination
in cracked nails no one will see.

Where, after all, to begin?
It is one thing, this life, and not another.
Silence, industry, too little trust.
Advance, decline, denial.
A bored house guest whose attention
turned elsewhere. An out-of-focus,
reached-for sepia-something.
It is the lost boy who knocks. His
leaden shoulders splinter
instead of those doors. It is
the bleeding woman who does not
make of herself a lover's bouquet.

Perhaps only those onions
pick their way through your private dark.
The onions you planted in warm, wet soil
shoot-side down, their white roots
flailing like feet.

spider song

My daughter watches the spiders weave
from the other side of a darkened window,
her pink snub nose inches from
rappelling monsters. Their bulbous flesh,
leather-dry as a swollen bog body,
bristles with hair like a great-aunt's
chin.
          And I tell her,
see the white fluff balls clinging to
the sill? Those are their babies.
Repelled, she backs off in
almost-mock horror, noting
the chick-soft of the nests and
flicking to the charred flesh
of the monster mothers.
She dangles her arms, regarding
their gangling length,
elbow creases, growing moles,
down fluff of wrist hair, and
sees how one may become the
other. I point out, too ardently,
the jewelled beauty of the
parent spider's strong web song and
move my mother-bulk into shadow,
recalling that today of all days
I forgot to shave my legs.

how skin remembers

In our blister-pink bath, bubbles pop
like untold tales. Languidly, you whisper,
tell me about China, mommy, and I think:
deboning a dragon is not like deboning a fish.
The thing has a tendency to stay alive,
accusing with a murky, blinking eye
like that rain-streaked face in the grimed window
above the furniture store in Guangzhou
one hot wet noon as we drove you all away.

Through tonight's steamed bathroom window
the glass-dappled sky wears its worn sun
like a shawl and tips backwards to a
squint-eyed past where nothing quite
pulls into focus but the winding smoke
from temple incense sticks, held aloft
in the fingers of a not-taken child whose
body is shaped like a question mark.

Digging for dinosaurs, you call them
dragons. Exotic red pandas have the face
of our garden raccoons and these bubbles
shatter like jack-hammered jade. One day,
my sky will fall, its whiteness crackmenting,
crashing to concrete like the bleached bones
of your never-dying dragon.

Tell me about China, you sing, curling
your child-spine against my wet skin
and settling bubble mounds on our four
knees like picture books. In our bath tonight
the eye of the dragon has closed

and we are safe in the only-present,
these bubbles tick-popping time bombs,
teetering Guilin wonders on the four peaks
of our weak knees. We both bear the burden
of "back then" and the threat of "someday soon,"
when the only possible stories
will be the ones too trapped for a telling,
cradled beneath the surface of your skin.

where the road ends

at the end of our road we found
Tadoussac and those whirling whales
that stirred the waves. A greedy gull
child-watched with slavered beak
as we turned our backs, homeward bound.
There were no birds at the end of that road,
no dip-soar seagull flight; just us, our child,
those miring dunes, and a red-eyed church
someone will recognize from our photos,
months too late, saying,
"my father went there."

Beyond the end of our road, a dark motel
where locals served congealed poutine,
poured scorn on our French, and wondered
at the Chinois child in words
they thought we could not understand.
"Oh, the places you'll go!" I will sigh
into next year's night, and she will ask us
boldly where the first road ended, was it
Tadoussac, on that end-of-season day
when everyone froze so momma
could see the whales and only momma
got to see the whales, stuck fast off starboard
in a mud-thick rain, while the gull-eyed girl
waited and someone asked the question:
where is the child from? The road ends here.
And starts. And ends. And starts. And
ends. And sometimes
starts again.

Notes and Acknowledgements

A number of these poems have previously appeared, in earlier forms, in *CV2*, *Event*, *Antigonish Review*, *Taddle Creek*, *This Magazine*, and the *Yorkshire Evening Post*. "Home Address" was the recipient of the annual Peace Poetry Prize in the UK.

The prose poem segment of "Threads" is constructed of dialogue and commentary from *Threads*, the 1984 BBC docudrama on the likely impact of nuclear fallout on the city of Sheffield, in the north of England.

The title "Nor Can Foot Feel, Being Shod" comes from a poem by Gerard Manley Hopkins.

"to: Fernando Castro Pacheco" is a found poem, inspired by phrases taken from a guide to the murals of Fernando Castro Pacheco, written by José Díaz Cervera.

This collection was made possible in part by a Writer's Reserve grant from the Ontario Arts Council.

About the Author

Julie Hartley has an MFA in Creative Writing from the University of British Columbia. Her novel for young adults, *The Finding Place*, was published in 2015 by Red Deer Press. Julie runs her own writing school in Toronto, hosts international creative writing retreats, and co-directs Centauri Summer Arts Camp, which brings together Canadian arts professionals and young people from all over the world. Originally from Lincolnshire, England, Julie lives in Toronto with her husband and daughter. Visit www.juliehartley.ca.

Selected Titles From Mansfield Press

Poetry

Tara Azzopardi, *Last Stop, Lonesome Town*
Nelson Ball, *In This Thin Rain*
Nelson Ball, *Some Mornings*
Nelson Ball, *Chewing Water*
Nelson Ball, *Walking*
Gary Barwin, *Moon Baboon Canoe*
Samantha Bernstein, *Spit on the Devil*
George Bowering, *Teeth: Poems 2006–2011*
Stephen Brockwell, *All of Us Reticent, Here, Together*
Stephen Brockwell, *Complete Surprising Fragments of Improbable Books*
Alice Burdick, *Book of Short Sentences*
Alice Burdick, *Flutter*
Alice Burdick, *Holler*
Sarah Burgoyne, *Saint Twin*
Jason Camlot, *What The World Said*
Laura Cok, *Doubter's Hymnal*
Pino Coluccio, *First Comes Love*
Marie-Ève Comtois, *My Planet of Kites*
Tim Conley, *Unless Acted Upon*
Dani Couture, *YAW*
Gary Michael Dault, *The Milk of Birds*
Frank Davey, *Poems Suitable to Current Material Conditions*
Adebe DeRango-Adem, *The Unmooring*
Pier Giorgio Di Cicco, *My Life Without Me*
Pier Giorgio Di Cicco, *Wishipedia*
Christopher Doda, *Aesthetics Lesson*
Christopher Doda, *Glutton for Punishment*
Glen Downie, *Monkey Soap*
Rishma Dunlop, *Lover Through Departure: New and Selected Poems*
Rishma Dunlop & Priscila Uppal, eds., *Red Silk: An Anthology of South Asian Women Poets*
Puneet Dutt, *The Better Monsters*
Laura Farina, *Some Talk of Being Human*
Paola Ferrante, *What To Wear When Surviving A Lion Attack*
Jaime Forsythe, *Sympathy Loophole*
Eva HD, *Rotten Perfect Mouth*
Eva HD, *Shiner*
James Hawes, *Breakfast with a Heron*
Jason Heroux, *Amusement Park of Constant Sorrow*
Jason Heroux, *Hard Work Cheering Up Sad Machines*
Jason Heroux, *Natural Capital*
John B. Lee, *In the Terrible Weather of Guns*
Joshua Levy, *The Loudest Thing*
D.A. Lockhart, *The Gravel Lot That Was Montana*
Jeanette Lynes, *The Aging Cheerleader's Alphabet*
David W. McFadden, *Abnormal Brain Sonnets*
David W. McFadden, *Be Calm, Honey*
David W. McFadden, *Shouting Your Name Down the Well: Tankas and Haiku*
David W. McFadden, *What's the Score?*
rob mclennan, *A halt, which is empty*
Kathryn Mockler, *The Purpose Pitch*
Nathaniel G. Moore, *Goodbye Horses*
Leigh Nash, *Goodbye, Ukulele*
Lillian Necakov, *The Bone Broker*
Lillian Necakov, *Hooligans*
Peter Norman, *At the Gates of the Theme Park*
Peter Norman, *Water Damage*
Natasha Nuhanovic, *Stray Dog Embassy*
Catherine Owen & Joe Rosenblatt, *Dog*
Corrado Paina, *Cinematic Taxi*
Nick Papaxanthos, *Love Me Tender*
Branka Petrovic, *Mechanics of a Gaze*
Shannon Quinn, *Nightlight for Children of Insomniacs*
Stuart Ross et al., *Our Days in Vaudeville*
Jim Smith, *Back Off, Assassin! New and Selected Poems*
Jim Smith, *Happy Birthday, Nicanor Parra*
Robert Earl Stewart, *Campfire Radio Rhapsody*
Meaghan Strimas, *Yes or Nope*
Meaghan Strimas & Priscila Uppal, *Another Dysfunctional Cancer Poem Anthology*
Carey Toane, *The Crystal Palace*
Aaron Tucker, *Punchlines*
Priscila Uppal, *Sabotage*
Priscila Uppal, *Summer Sport: Poems*
Priscila Uppal, *Winter Sport: Poems*
Priscila Uppal, *On Second Thought*
Steve Venright, *Floors of Enduring Beauty*
Brian Wickers, *Stations of the Lost*
Tara-Michelle Ziniuk, *Whatever, Iceberg*

Fiction

Marianne Apostolides, *The Lucky Child*
Sarah Dearing, *The Art of Sufficient Conclusions*
Salvatore Difalco, *Mean Season*
Paula Eisenstein, *Flip Turn*
Sara Heinonen, *Dear Leaves, I Miss You All*
Jason Heroux, *Amusement Park of Constant Sorrow*
Kasia Jaronczyk, *Lemons*
Christine Miscione, *Carafola*
Marko Sijan, *Mongrel*
Tom Walmsley, *Dog Eat Rat*
Corinne Wasilewski, *Live from the Underground*

Non-Fiction

George Bowering, *How I Wrote Certain of My Books*
Mark Cirilo, *Pizza Cultura*
Pier Giorgio Di Cicco, *Municipal Mind: Manifestos for the Creative City*
Amy Lavender Harris, *Imagining Toronto*
David W. McFadden, *Mother Died Last Summer*

For a complete list of Mansfield Press titles, please visit mansfieldpress.net